DR. MYLES

KEYS *for* VISION

w

WHITAKER
HOUSE

KEYS FOR VISION

ISBN: 978-1-60374-153-8
Printed in the United States of America
© 2009 by Dr. Myles Munroe

Dr. Myles Munroe
Bahamas Faith Ministries International
P.O. Box N9583
Nassau, Bahamas
E-mail: bfmadmin@bfmmm.com
www.bfmmm.com; www.bfmi.tv; www.mylesmunroe.tv

Whitaker House
1030 Hunt Valley Circle
New Kensington, PA 15068
www.whitakerhouse.com

1 2 3 4 5 6 7 8 9 10 11 12 **ШУ** 17 16 15 14 13 12 11 10 09

INTRODUCTION

*G*od created each person with a unique vision that no one else can accomplish. Your dreams, talents, and desires can be refined in a process of discovering and completing your life's purpose so that your special gifts to this world can shine forth.

Vision is a conception that is inspired by God in the heart of a human. What have you always wanted to do? What is your dream? What is your heart's desire? When you can begin to see your vision clearly, you will be able to fulfill the purpose for your life.

Keys for Vision reveals the nature of purpose so that you can capture your own personal vision. It provides key principles to help you understand the mind-set, tools, and skills necessary to bring your vision into reality.

The gift of vision is greater than the gift of sight. Sight is a function of the eyes, but vision is a function of the heart. The power of vision is that your future is not just ahead of you—it also lies within you.

—*Dr. Myles Munroe*

KEYS for VISION

$\mathcal{D}$o you have a sense of personal purpose? Do you get up every day with a feeling of anticipation because you know you're doing what you were born to do?

Have you secretly thought you were meant to do something significant in life, but you don't know what it is?

$\mathcal{M}$any of us do not reflect who we truly are. We are living as clay vessels when, in reality, we are pure gold inside. This gold is the dreams we have for our lives that are not yet reality, the talents that we have not yet developed, and the purposes for our lives that are not yet fulfilled.

What is your dream? What do you imagine yourself doing? What do you want to accomplish?

KEYS for VISION

$\mathcal{N}$othing noble or noteworthy
on earth was ever done without vision.
No invention, development, or great
feat was ever accomplished without
vision's inspiring power.

$\mathcal{O}$ur world today is in desperate need of vision. We need visionaries who can see beyond the now into a preferred future, who have the skill to transfer that vision into reality, and who have the courage to inspire us to go there.

When you have no vision, you will simply relive the past with its disappointments and failures. Therefore, vision is the key to your future.

*V*ision doesn't try to recapture the good old days; rather, it desires to create days that have not yet existed. We need to build on the past, but we cannot return to it.

$\mathscr{V}$ision sets you free from the
limitations of what the eyes can see and
allows you to enter into the liberty of
what the heart can feel.

Having a purpose and vision has to do with your life existence. It enables you to answer the question, "Why was I born?"

$\mathcal{Y}$ou can know why you exist,
and you can experience a remarkable life
in light of that knowledge. Life doesn't
have to be an aimless, repetitive exercise.
You were meant to be going somewhere,
to be headed toward a destination.

*I*t is more important to know why you were born than to know the fact that you were born. To fulfill your vision, you must have a clear guiding purpose for your life. Clarity of purpose will keep you from being distracted by nonessentials.

$\mathscr{P}$urpose is when you know and understand what you were born to accomplish. Vision is when you can see it in your mind by faith and begin to imagine it.

*H*aving a vision, or a dream, is inherent in being human. God not only created each person on earth with a distinct design, but He also placed in everyone a unique vision to give purpose and meaning to life.

$\mathcal{T}$rue vision is not a human invention.
It's about the desires God imparts to us.
Vision is what God wants us to contribute
in building His kingdom on earth.

We learn to discern true vision through our relationship with God and by reading His Word, because genuine vision is always in alignment with His nature and character. If an idea is not in keeping with God's will, set it aside.

$\mathcal{M}$any people have been looking for God's will everywhere except in themselves. To find your vision, you have to look within yourself, where God has placed it. God's will is as close to us as our most persistent thoughts and deepest desires.

$\mathcal{N}$o matter how old you grow, the same thoughts and desires will keep coming back to you. This is because the will of God for you never changes.

Whether you are twenty, sixty, or ninety years old, there is a burden within you, a "responsible urge" to carry out all that you were designed to do. It is a cry of the heart—a cry of purpose that says, "I was born to do something that I must fulfill."

Without a vision of the future, life loses its meaning. An absence of meaning then leads to a lack of hope. Vision is the key to life because where there's a dream, there's hope, and where there's hope, there's faith—and faith is the substance, or fulfillment, of what you are hoping for.

A vision is real when it is the only thing that gives you true satisfaction. Going to work is a dismal experience for many people because they are doing something they hate. It is God's desire for us to enjoy our work, but this can happen only when we're doing the right work.

People have all kinds of ideas in their minds, but they rarely act on them. While the poorest person in the world is a person without a dream, the most frustrated person in the world is someone who has a dream but doesn't know how to bring it to pass.

Whatever your hand finds to do, do it with all your might" (Ecclesiastes 9:10). The vision in your heart is the spark that will enable you to pursue your dream because, unless you do so with all your enthusiasm and strength, it will not happen.

$\mathcal{E}$very person is a leader in his or her own vision, because that person is the only one who can imagine, nurture, and fulfill it.

*A*lthough we are all born as originals, most of us become imitators. You are not to mimic the gifts of others. You should be so busy stirring up your own gift that you don't have time to be jealous of anyone else or to feel sorry for yourself.

*I*f you want to know where you're supposed to go in life, you have to establish a connection with the Person who gave you the assignment, who created you. When you love God with all your heart, soul (will), mind, and strength, He reveals to you the assignment you were born to fulfill.

The very substance of life is for you to find God's purpose and fulfill it. Until you do that, you are not really alive. Discovering something you can put your whole self into will fill your life with new hope and purpose. It will give you a reason for living.

One person with vision is more powerful than the passive force of ninety-nine people who are merely interested in doing or becoming something.

*Y*ou are the sum total of the choices and decisions you make every day. You can choose to stay where you are right now, or you can choose to move forward in life by pursuing your dream. Take your life out of neutral. God has given you the power and the responsibility to achieve your life's vision.

*M*ost people do things because they have to. Wouldn't you like to do things because you have decided to, based on your purpose?

$\mathcal{V}$ision is the primary motivator of human action, and, therefore, everything we do should be because of the vision God has placed in our hearts. Vision influences the way you conduct your entire life, such as what you spend your time and money on and what your priorities are.

"Where there is no vision, the people perish" (Proverbs 29:18 KJV). These words capture the significant role that vision has in our individual, corporate, and national lives. Where there is no revelation of the future, people throw off self-control, personal discipline, and restraint. Simply put, vision is the source of personal and corporate discipline.

Vision is the juice of life. It is the prerequisite for passion and the source of persistence. When you have vision, you know how to stay in the race and complete it.

When a person receives an idea from God, it must be cultivated soon or the idea often goes away. It's not just having ideas that is important. Ideas need plans if they are going to become reality.

No person can give you your vision. It is God-given. You can go to as many seminars as possible and receive all kinds of wonderful instruction, but no one except God can give you the idea that you were born to fulfill.

God is not only the Author of your vision but also your continuing Support as you progress toward its fulfillment. If you stay in touch with God, you will always be nourished in both life and vision.

As long as a person can hold on to his vision, then there is always a chance for him to move out of his present circumstances and toward the fulfillment of his purpose.

$\mathcal{N}$o matter how big the world is, there's a place for you in it when you discover and manifest your gift. *"A man's gift makes room for him, and brings him before great men"* (Proverbs 18:16 NKJV). You were designed to be known for your gift. It is this gift that will enable you to fulfill your vision.

*I*f you do things in a halfway manner, you will probably always be able to find some sort of job. It is when you decide that you're going to discover something that is truly yours that you will find your gift, fulfill your vision, and be remembered by others.

$\mathcal{M}$any people are working for money.
That's an inferior reason to work. We
must work for the visions within us.
Whenever you exercise your gift, the
world will not only make room for you,
but it will also pay you for it.

I remind you to stir up the gift of God which is in you" (2 Timothy 1:6 NKJV). You stir up your gift by developing, refining, enhancing, and using it.

*E*ducation can't give you your gift, but it can help you to develop it so that it can be used to the maximum. No one else can activate your gift for you. You have to do it yourself.

We read in the Bible that God went to people who were already past retirement age, and He recharged them. They have become noteworthy in history because they started over when others (and even they themselves) thought their lives were almost over. If you believe you're too old to use your gift, you are believing a lie.

$\mathscr{Y}$our gift will give you your youth back. Your gift will give you energy and strength. You'll be healthier. You'll stop talking about dying and start talking about living.

God loves dreamers. He gives visions, and He is attracted to people who love to dream big. Don't forget that you are unique, special, and irreplaceable. You are not meant to be like anyone else.

What is the difference between the dreamer who realizes his dream and the dreamer whose dream becomes a nightmare of unfulfilled hopes? The dreamer who succeeds is someone who has a clear vision and acts on it.

 $\mathcal{V}$ ision always emanates from purpose. Why? God is the Author of vision, and it is His nature to be purposeful in everything He does. He first institutes a purpose, and then He creates someone or something to fulfill that purpose.

$\mathcal{G}$od has given us birth for a purpose, and as far as He is concerned, that purpose is already finished because He has placed within us the potential for fulfilling it. We can see that purpose through faith. Only by seeing what is not yet here can you bring something new, creative, and exciting into existence.

You are not an experiment. God wouldn't have allowed you to start your life and your purpose unless they were already completed in eternity.

To have vision means to see something coming into view as if it were already there. God wants you to "see" the completion of your vision by knowing that He already planned and established it before you were born. Vision is therefore "foresight with insight based on hindsight."

Whatever you were born to do, God has assigned a season in which it is to be done—and that season is the duration of your life. It is crucial for you to have a vision because your purpose can be fulfilled only during the time you are given on earth to accomplish it.

$\mathcal{G}$od essentially completed us before He created us. Not only does He establish our ends, but He also gives us glimpses of them through the visions He puts in our hearts. We must pay attention to His work within us so that we can understand more of what He *"has done from beginning to end"* (Ecclesiastes 3:11).

Your end doesn't look anything like your beginning—or like any other point in the process. This is why you must live by faith, looking forward with expectation for what God has already completed; otherwise, you will believe only what you see with your physical eyes rather than the vision you see in your heart.

*A*t the time when we recognize our visions, we are usually not ready for them. We don't yet have the ability to handle the big things that we're dreaming. We don't have the experience or the character for them. God prepares us to receive and work in our visions.

KEYS for VISION

*O*ur jobs can serve a purpose in God's plan. He places us in jobs that will prepare us for our life's work. Submit yourself to your job, learn what you're supposed to learn, and get all the knowledge that you can from it, because you're going to move on in a little while.

KEYS for VISION

You never have to worry if you are able to fulfill your life's vision. God always gives us the ability to do whatever He calls us to do. The fact that you were created to complete it means that you have everything you need to accomplish it.

*I*f you have gotten off track in life, it doesn't matter how young or old you are; refocus on your vision and make decisions that will lead you there. Say to God, "I know I haven't made the best use of my time in the past, but I'm going to make the rest of my life count."

*Y*our vision is a clear conception of
something that is not yet reality,
but which can exist. It is a strong
image of a preferable future.

*I*f you are unclear about your vision, ask God to reveal to you the deepest desires He has placed within you.

*V*ision isn't essentially about us—it's about God. *"Many are the plans in a man's heart, but it is the Lord's purpose that prevails"* (Proverbs 19:21). True vision is about the desires God imparts to us. It is not our private view of the future; rather, it is the view of our future inspired by God.

Sometimes, God's ideas come in multiples. He may put five or six things in your mind that He wants you to do, each one for a different season of your life.

$\mathscr{T}$he specifics of your plans may change as your purpose unfolds, but your purpose is permanent. No matter what happens in life, you'll never get away from what God has put in your heart to do.

KEYS for VISION

$\mathcal{M}$any of us have been trained to dream small and not try to do anything too big. When we compare what we are told in the "real" world with our own dreams, our visions seem unrealistic. Yet if a vision is truly from God, we are meant to continue on, no matter what the difficulty.

*T*rue success is not in what you accomplish; it is in doing what God told you to do.

A true vision should always focus on helping humanity in some way—building others up rather than pulling them down. Likewise, vision should be accompanied by compassion. You need to be careful and sensitive not to hurt anyone on the way to achieving your purpose.

Your perspective on your finances should be God-centered, not self-centered. Treat your finances as a resource God has provided to fulfill your vision, not as a tool to fill your life with luxuries.

*G*oing against your purpose may be a personal issue, but it's never a private one. Your obedience to your vision affects not only your life, but also the lives of those who will work with you to fulfill it.

If we are in line with God's nature and character, we will desire what He desires, and we will be fulfilled in a way we never could have been by following our own ambitions.

A sense of personal vision is often birthed within a broader vision, and it will also be fulfilled in the context of a larger purpose. God wants you to bring your time, energy, resources, and creative power to be part of a larger vision to which your vision is connected.

*N*o great work was ever done by just one person. You don't receive your vision from other people, but you are enabled to fulfill it through others. The leader of a corporate vision "draws out" the personal visions of those in the group by helping them to activate their passions, dreams, gifts, and talents.

KEYS for VISION

$\mathscr{G}$od brings the corporate vision
into your life not to give you vision,
which He has already given you, but
to stir up your personal vision.

We must have an attitude of cooperation with those with whom we share a corporate vision. Fulfilling your vision includes not trying to undermine people or letting jealousy get in the way of the corporate vision. It means working with others in a productive way.

*I*f you and I are part of the same corporate vision, then I need your vision, and you need mine. Therefore, we must work together. We are not to isolate ourselves in our private successes.

$\mathscr{A}$re you starting to think differently? Are you beginning to dream? Are you able to believe in the possibility of things you never thought possible before? Then you have started to catch the vision for your life.

People fail because they don't know what they want to succeed in. A vision is a very precise statement that has a specific emphasis and definable boundaries. You must choose where you want to go in life and then be decisive and faithful in carrying it out.

God created you for a purpose, and that purpose is supposed to be your focus. When we aim at everything, we usually hit nothing. When a person tries to do everything, he ends up becoming a "jack-of-all-trades and master of none."

$\mathcal{D}$reaming is only the beginning of vision. We should have wills rather than mere wishes. Instead of wishing that things would get better, we must make concrete resolutions and carry them out.

$\mathcal{M}$any people's visions never take specific shape because they can't make up their minds what they want to do in life. The most miserable people in the world are those who can never make a decision. Prolonged indecisiveness is a vision-killer and drains the joy out of life.

KEYS for VISION

$\mathcal{S}$ome people have trouble carrying their visions through to the end because they are "professional starters." They're always beginning something, but they never finish anything. Everything you leave unfinished will discourage you from completing other projects. The unfinished has a way of haunting your life.

What do you think is your greatest obstacle to pursuing and completing your vision? What steps can you take to begin overcoming that obstacle?

When you have several gifts and talents, focus on one or two of them and stir them up. Don't allow multiple gifts to distract you from taking specific steps toward fulfilling your vision.

$\mathcal{N}$ot everybody will understand your vision. Some people will try to talk you out of your plan, saying, "You can't do that!" If you listen to them, you will throw your plan away and end up an average person, like they are. People who are going nowhere like to take others with them.

*I*f you set a destination for your
life and make a plan to move toward
what you desire, while continuing to pray
about your vision, God will guide you
where you need to go.

Have you expressed to God what is in your heart, and have you presented Him with your plan for accomplishing it? You can't fulfill your dream by yourself. You must have God's help. When you put your plan on paper, you will find that you have plenty of material for your prayers.

You are not defined by your past or confined by external factors. Your purpose is greater than your failures and mistakes. God has a good purpose and definite plan for your life despite what your background is or what mistakes you have made.

*I*f God tells you to build, start,
invest, create, or manufacture something,
then it will bother you deep inside
until you take action on it.

*I*f you are afraid to take action to
move toward your vision, consider this:
It is better to make a decision that will prove
to be wrong, but which you can learn from,
than not to make any decision at all. People
who succeed *try*. People who don't try
have no chance of success.

*I*n order to find your vision, you must be in touch with the values and priorities of the kingdom of God.

When you are deciding on a vision, don't sell yourself short. Your vision should be something that lives on after you're gone, something that has greater lasting power than possessions.

A true visionary irritates those who want things to remain as they always have. Vision is always pushing the envelope. It demands change by its very nature.

God gave us the gift of imagination to keep us from focusing only on our present conditions.

A clear vision gives us a passion that keeps us continually moving forward in life.

You will never be successful in your vision until you truly understand your potential. Your potential is determined by the assignment God has given you to do. Whatever you were born to do, you are equipped to do.

$\mathcal{P}$otential is hidden capacity, untapped power, unreleased energy. It is all you could be but haven't yet become. Your imagination isn't big enough for all God wants to do for you.

*Y*our ability isn't dependent on what you perceive as your limitations. You are perfect for your purpose.

Now to him who is able to do immeasurably more than all we ask or imagine, according to his power that is at work within us" (Ephesians 3:20). The mighty power of God's Spirit who lives inside you will enable you to fulfill the vision He has given you.

The ability to accomplish your vision is manifested when you say yes to your dream and obey God.

God will never call you to do something that He hasn't already given you the ability to do or that He won't give you the ability to do when the time comes.

$\mathcal{G}$od reveals our potential as we act on our dreams. Starting with what you already have makes your vision successful because God will take care of the rest.

Vision is the precedent for passion. Passion means that, no matter how tough things are, what you believe is bigger than what you see. Passion keeps you focused on your vision.

There is no way any of us can move toward our dreams without a plan. A vision becomes a plan when it is captured, fleshed out, and written down.

*I*f you don't have a plan for your life, you have nothing to refer to when you want to make sure you are on track.

Keys for Vision

When ideas are cultivated, they become imagination. Imagination, if it is watered and developed, becomes a plan. Finally, if a plan is followed, it becomes a reality.

You must have a clear idea of your own identity in God. Many of us have become what other people want us to be. We have not yet discovered our unique, irreplaceable identity. Yet it is knowing your true identity that gives you the courage to write your life plan.

Your dream is worth writing down.
If God gave it to you, it deserves to be
done. When you write down a plan, it's a
description of the end of your life,
not the beginning.

When you write your vision, realize that it won't be a finished product. You will keep refining it as God makes your purpose clearer as the months and years go by, and as you experience spiritual and personal growth.

God gives us dreams to deliver us from mediocrity. Passionate people are those who have discovered something more important than life itself.

Persistence will keep you moving forward, yet you need passion to feed your persistence. You must put your whole heart into your vision.

*P*hysical sight is the ability to see things as they are. Vision is the capacity to see things as they could be, and that takes faith. When we have vision, we are governed by the faith God has put in our hearts.

*I*deas are so powerful that many
nations are ruled by the thoughts
of men who have long since died.

KEYS for VISION

While thoughts are the most important things on earth, words are the most powerful. Thoughts design a future, but words create that future.

Whether words are spoken or written, they are full of creative power. When you speak words expressing what you see in your vision, your words become creative power to help bring that vision to fruition.

The faith of vision is crucial because the way you see things determines how you think and act and, therefore, whether or not your vision will become reality. You can undermine your vision through negative thoughts and words.

God has a plan for each of our lives, yet He brings those plans to pass in a gradual way. There is no hurried way to get to God's vision.

The process of vision develops
our character and produces
responsibility in us.

$\mathcal{S}$ometimes, we think that just because we're going through difficult times, God has stopped working to fulfill our purposes. Yet God is working on us, preparing us for our purposes through the process.

*L*ife's hardships are part of God's perfect plan for us and our visions. Live by faith as you move through the process of vision.

*P*rioritize your life in keeping with your vision. Prioritizing creates useful limits on your choices. Yes and no are the most powerful words you will ever say.

KEYS for VISION

Setting priorities is the key to effective decision-making. When you see your destination, it helps you to discipline your life in ways that train, prepare, and provide for your vision.

$\mathcal{S}$omething is beneficial if it relates to what you want to accomplish and takes you to your goal. Ask yourself, "What benefits me? What will move me toward my preferable future?"

Your greatest challenge is not in choosing between good or bad but between good and best.

For any true vision that you have, God has people prepared to work with you, and they will be a blessing to you.

You become like those with whom you spend time. Choose friends who are going in the same direction as you. Spend time with people of vision.

$\mathcal{B}$e careful whom you allow to influence you because your vision will be either encouraged or destroyed by others. People have the potential to create your environment. Your environment then determines your mind-set, and your mind-set determines your future.

Protect your mental environment.
Spend major time with positive influences
and minor time with negative influences.
Priority requires that there are people
and places that you are going to have to
disassociate yourself from if you're going
to make it to your dream.

God often gives us dreams that confound us at first because He wants to make sure we don't attempt to fulfill them apart from Him. Our provisions are never equal to our visions at the moment we receive them. Our provisions are usually hidden until we act on our visions.

*I*t is our job to understand, believe, and write down our visions while it is God's responsibility to explain how He's going to accomplish them in His own time. That frees us to be creative and productive in pursuing our visions.

Prosperity doesn't mean that tomorrow's need is met today, but that today's need is met today. True prosperity means to be free of worry and fear and reflects a state of contentedness that everything necessary is being taken care of by God.

God has designed every purpose with its own prosperity. Your purpose has built-in provision for it. God never requires from you what He does not already have in reserve for you. Clean out your heavenly warehouse. Daily, ask God, "Deliver to me what I need today."

Cultivate what is around you and make it a resource for your vision.

*E*very true vision will be tested for authenticity. If your vision is authentic, life is going to try it, just to make sure.

Life has been tough for some of us from the time we were children. No matter what your background is, your relationship with your Father in heaven will help you to overcome your difficult circumstances and to fulfill your purpose as His child.

*L*et opposition strengthen you rather than stop you. The vision in your heart needs to be larger than any opposition that comes against you so you can persist in your life's purpose.

*O*pposition is often proof that you are doing something significant with your life. Don't sacrifice your dreams because of a fear of conflict or disagreement. People who change the world have declared independence from other people's expectations.

Keys for Vision

$\mathscr{D}$estiny demands diligence. Many people lose because they quit when life says no the first time, but persistent people win. They never take no for an answer when it comes to their visions.

Courage is the ability to stand up in the face of fear. Fear is a positive thing when it gives birth to courage. If you're afraid to step out in your vision because it's so big, then let your courage come to life as you trust God. The impossible is always possible with God.

The light of God's vision in your heart is stronger and brighter than any darkness in this world.

Character is formed by pressure.
The purpose of pressure is to get rid
of what is not of God and to leave
what is pure gold.

*Y*ou cannot rush a vision. It is given by God, and He will carry it out in His own time. Your vision will come to pass if you are willing to progress at the vision's pace.

*V*ision takes time and patience and often involves change. Patience is the key to having power over adversity and turmoil. When you are patient in the fulfillment of your vision, you are able to be calm in the midst of uncertainty.

*E*ven though there will be times of stress, disappointment, and pressure, the vision *will* come to pass. It is not a matter of whether the vision is going to be fulfilled; it's a matter of whether you're going to be true to it in the midst of trials so that God can bring it to pass.

There is no stopping a person who understands that pressure can be good for him, because pressure is one of the keys to perseverance.

Keys for Vision

*A*re you willing to pay the
price for your vision?

To be successful in your vision, you must have a daily, dynamic, personal prayer life with God. Prayer sustains us in the demands of vision. God will bring you through your difficulties and give you the victory through prayer based on His Word.

$\mathcal{P}$rayer is the essential resource of vision. Remain connected to your Source for the renewal of your purpose, faith, and strength, and you will be able to persevere to the fulfillment of your vision.

$\mathcal{G}$od is the One who planted your life's purpose within you in the beginning. He has invested Himself in your dream, and He will bring it to pass.

*Y*ou were born to achieve something significant, and you were destined to make a difference in your generation. Reconnect with your passion; your vision awaits your action.

*O*ur lives are like seed. We were born with the potential for the fulfillment of our destinies, which have already been established within us. Plant the seed of your vision by beginning to act on it, and then nurture it by faith. Your vision will develop until it is fully grown and bears much fruit.

In what ways will you
begin to "plant the seed" of
your vision today?

We were born to do something in life that leaves nutrients for the seeds of the next generation to take root in and grow.

$\mathcal{D}$o you know what you want to do next week, next month, next year, five years from now? Do you have a plan for the next twenty years of your life? God has given you a mind, the gift of imagination, the anointing of the Holy Spirit, and the vision of faith. What are you waiting for?

$\mathscr{N}$ever expect anything less than the highest you can go after. Always expect more than what you have, more than what you are currently doing. Dream big. Somewhere inside you there is always the ability to dream. No matter how challenging things get, don't give up, because *your vision is the key to fulfilling your life's purpose.*

156

Make your life on earth
count—for yourself and others.

ABOUT THE AUTHOR

Dr. Myles Munroe is an international motivational speaker, best-selling author, educator, leadership mentor, and consultant for government and business. Traveling extensively throughout the world, Dr. Munroe addresses critical issues affecting the full range of human, social, and spiritual development. The central theme of his message is the transformation of followers into leaders and the maximization of individual potential.

Founder and president of Bahamas Faith Ministries International (BFMI), a multidimensional organization headquartered in Nassau, Bahamas, Dr. Munroe is also the founder and executive producer of a number of radio and television programs aired worldwide. He has a B.A. from Oral Roberts University and an M.A. from the University of Tulsa and has been awarded a number of honorary doctoral degrees.

Dr. Munroe and his wife, Ruth, travel as a team and are involved in teaching seminars together. Both are leaders who minister with sensitive hearts and international vision. They are the proud parents of two college graduates, Charisa and Chairo (Myles Jr.).

For Information on Religious Tourism
e-mail: ljohnson@bahamas.com
1.800.224.3681

www.worship.bahamas.com

These inspirational quotes from best-selling author Dr. Myles Munroe
on leadership, single living, marriage, and prayer can be applied
to your life in powerful and practical ways.

Keys for Leadership: ISBN: 978-1-60374-029-6 • Gift • 160 pages
Keys for Living Single: ISBN: 978-1-60374-032-6 • Gift • 160 pages
Keys for Marriage: ISBN: 978-1-60374-030-2 • Gift • 160 pages
Keys for Prayer: ISBN: 978-1-60374-031-9 • Gift • 160 pages

WHITAKER
HOUSE